From words to sales:The StorySelling Method for Captivating Customers and Closing Deal

James L. Smith

INTRODUCTION

The power of words in sales

Welcome to a reality where a solitary word might open entryways, a very much created sentence can change the course of a business, and correspondence is the way to deal with achievement.

At the time, I remember working as a sales representative for a software company. Our organization had recently delivered another item and was restless to change over leads into deals. Our manager, Sarah, called us together for a session of creative thinking to come up with efficient strategies.

Mark, one of my associates, introduced an astonishing individual encounter that empowered every one of us. He enlightened us concerning his adoration for traveling and how he habitually became mixed up in nature. During that time, he relied upon a compass and a guide to direct him back to somewhere safe and secure. My considerations were lighted by Imprint's record.

I offered that we utilize a comparative thought in our deals strategy. We expected to give our potential shoppers a compass and a guide to assist them with exploring from their underlying interest in our item to making a buy. Sarah preferred the idea and encouraged us to foster it further.

We split our deals cycle into unmistakable stages and fabricated a guide-like visual portrayal of it. Each step was joined by exact achievements and activities that were expected to continue. The principal stage, for instance, was "Mindfulness," in which we attempted to catch the consideration of expected clients through centered advertising efforts

We made intensive item leaflets, astute blog pieces, and connected with online entertainment content to assist them with tracking down their direction. Clients were guided by these resources to the advantages and value of our product. We made it a highlight to make sense of how our item could lighten their concerns and make their life more straightforward.

We provided our shoppers with additional devices and assets as they continued through each level to fulfill their singular requirements. From customized consultations and case studies to free trials and product demonstrations, we were committed to making their experience as simple as possible.

Our outreach group viewed the compass and guide method as a distinct advantage. We not only generated more leads but also successfully nurtured them, which led to a significant increase in conversions. We fastidiously followed our headway, making changes en route relying upon client information and market patterns.

Our director Sarah introduced some superb news months after the fact during a group meeting. Our company had exceeded all previous sales goals and set new sales records. She praised our innovative strategy and credited our success to the compass and map method. Seeing how our insignificant anecdote had grown into a realistic and effective sales strategy was very satisfying.

The compass and guide turned into a fundamental piece of our deals cycle from there on out. It advised us that every potential client had their own outing to take, and it was our commitment to help them through it bit by bit until they settled on a certain buying choice. It filled in as an unmistakable update that great deals request more than basic words; they require a very much created street and a reasonable course.

Chapter1

The Art of Persuasion

Any business's ability to generate revenue and achieve success is largely dependent on sales. Experts in deals should get a handle on the specialty of influence. Influence is the capacity to convince individuals to change their perspectives, sentiments, and choices, like making a buy. While certain individuals seem, by all accounts, to be normal sales reps, in all actuality viable influence abilities can be considered, rehearsed, and moved along.

This broad aide will dig into the intricacies of deal's influence. We will take a gander at the brain research of influence, the need of compatibility, significant selling procedures, and moral issues while impacting expected clients. Toward the finish of this conversation, you will have acquired critical bits of knowledge that will empower you to turn into an expert deals persuader.

The Influence Brain science

Understanding the mental ideas that oversee human direction is fundamental for figuring out the craft of influence in deals. A few speculations give light on how individuals' choices are impacted:

a.The Rule of Correspondence: Individuals frequently feel committed to return leans toward and respond to good ways of behaving. Giving worth or advantages prior to requesting something as a trade off would improve the probability of a deal.

b. Social Evidence: People are influenced by the actions and choices of other people, especially by those who appear to be influential or similar to them. Utilizing tributes, contextual investigations, or web-based entertainment to show the ubiquity of an item or administration can valuably affect likely buyers.

c. Legitimacy: Individuals are bound to heed the guidance of seen specialists or specialists. Creating notoriety and information in your subject can extraordinarily upgrade your enticing endeavors.

d. Shortage: When confronted with confined accessibility or selective arrangements, individuals' apprehension about passing up a major opportunity (FOMO) urges them to rapidly act. Making a feeling of shortage can fabricate direness, inciting expected purchasers to settle on a speedy choice.

Building Connections: The Premise of Influence

Prior to endeavoring to convince somebody to get, making compatibility and a veritable connection is basic. To comprehend their clients' necessities and agony spots, deal experts should focus on undivided attention and compassion. You lay out an environment in which potential purchasers are more open to your convincing information by fostering a relationship based on trust and understanding.

Selling Procedures That Are Fundamental

a. Message Personalization: In deals, a one-size-fits-all system seldom works. Customize your pitch to every client's novel necessities, interests, and inspirations. This tweaked touch shows that you really care about their singular requirements.

a. Narrating: We are designed to associate with stories. Utilize an account to show how your item or administration has helped different clients. You draw in likely shoppers' feelings and make your deal more vital by depicting a dazzling picture of progress or change.

c. Posing Unassuming Inquiries: By asking questions that are open-ended and elicit meaningful responses, you can encourage consumer discussion. You might meet their prerequisites all the more really and change your convincing methodology by empowering them to offer their viewpoints and concerns.

d. Complaints Taking care of: Expect and determine possible protests before they happen. Readiness is fundamental for overseeing complaints with certainty, showing your ability, and changing over worries into selling possibilities.

a. Making a Need to keep moving: As recently expressed, shortage can incite activity. To tempt possible buyers to act rapidly, utilize restricted time offers, selective limits, or other time-delicate motivating forces.

f. Preliminary terminations: Use preliminary terminations to gauge the client's advantage and responsiveness all through the deals cycle. These are kind comments or questions that let you test the waters and adjust your approach as necessary.

g. Securing and outlining: Your product's value or pricing may be perceived differently by potential customers if presented in a particular context. The proposition can be made more enticing by securing the cost to a higher-esteem thing or depicting it as an insignificant month to month charge.

Influence Moral Contemplations

Influence is an amazing asset, however it should be utilized shrewdly and morally. Among the main contemplations are:

a. Straightforwardness: Tell the truth and clear about the abilities and restrictions of your item or administration. Deluding clients might bring about transient benefits, however it will at last subvert your standing and long haul execution.

b. Independence: Influence ought not be mistaken for control. Regard expected purchasers' independence and try not to drive them towards choices they are awkward with.

c. Long haul associations: Instead of zeroing in on transient benefits, focus on long haul associations with clients. Clients who are fulfilled are bound to become committed promoters and rehash purchasers.

To sum up, the specialty of influence in deals is a multi-layered expertise that requires information on human brain research, compelling correspondence, and moral contemplations. You can emphatically further develop your abilities to sell by laying out compatibility, redoing your words, and applying key strategies. Remember that moral influence prompts deals achievement, yet in addition to long haul organizations and an ideal standing in the commercial center. You might open the key to fruitful selling in the steadily impacting business world by continuously improving your convincing abilities and zeroing in on creating an incentive for your purchasers.

1.1 Psychology of Influence

The brain research of impact investigates the psyche processes that influence our choices and ponders how advertisers might make use of this data to their advantage. This article gives knowledge into the specialty of influence by diving into the essential ideas and systems of impact brain research.

•Reciprocity: The Giving and entering. Power Correspondence is an abecedarian rule of effect. Individuals significantly need to repay when they gain a product of worth. This section looks at how advertisers can use the power of correspondence to their advantage by providing implied visitors with free samples, discounts, or useful content. By including the standard of correspondence, advertisers can convey a sense of gratitude and alleviate the burden of generating the ideal response.

•Others' Affect Social Proof
As amicable animals, we consistently search for direction from others while making sentiments. Social proof emphasizes the direct influence of

other people's perspectives on our own. This section analyzes how publicists can use social confirmation for their possible advantage by showing spectators, customer overviews, and imprints. Sponsors can encourage trust and legitimacy by displaying that others have had incredible guests with a thing or organization, which prompts extended deals.

• Depending on the Calling.
Individuals have a trademark tendency to regard and notice authority numbers. This section looks at how promoters can use power for their expected advantage by showing secure subject matter experts or using hotshot marks. Promoters can impact customer geste

by interfacing their things or organizations with authoritative individuals who are known for their trust and data.

•The Dread about Missing a significant open door Due to frustration. The failure rule takes use of our anxiety toward missing wonderful openings. This part looks at how sponsors could use confined time levels, specific decreases, or limited form things to make a need to continue to move and disillusionment around their immolations. Sponsors can augment deals by imitating fear of adversity in guests and convincing them to act snappily.

•Thickness People have a saturated drive to act in simultaneousness with their viewpoints, values, and tone-picture. This section looks at how promoters can use thickness for their possible advantage by mentioning bitsy obligations from specific guests. Publicists can encourage an illustration of thickness and lift the gamble of unborn plans by beginning with minor exhibitions equivalent as purchasing it up for a notice or going to a web-based class.

•**Getting ready and planning**
The primary information gave to us ceaselessly influences our choices and evaluations. This part plunges into the misrepresentations of getting and planning, as well as how might use them to

affect purchaser prints. By intentionally outlining data, laying out cutting edge beginning costs, or preparing with positive affiliations, advertisers can impact buyer decisions and raise the apparent worth of their administrations.

•Significant suppliances feelings have a critical part in decision stumble, persistently booting sufficiency. This part examines the ampleness of significant petitions to God in advancing and deals. By evoking emotions like joy, dread, pity, or compassion in customers, advertisers can build personal connections with them, leading to fewer commitments and arrangements.

•**Framing and Strong Language.**
How data is placed and deciphered can be essentially impacted by the way things are conveyed. This part looks at how to impact purchaser sees by using authoritative language and framing systems. Sponsors can impact customer stations and lift the commitment of a purchase by centering benefits, pushing uncommon selling components, and illustrating

illuminating in a positive light. impact mind research gives accommodating perceptivity into the unpredictable cycles that impact client geste

additionally, decision wood. Promoters could create persuading dispatches and impact purchaser choices by getting it and rehearsing cerebral comprehensive articulations equivalent as correspondence, social evidence, authority, frustration, thickness, getting, significant requests, and mental inspirations. Anyway, these ways ought to be counterbalanced with moral examinations, ensuring lucidity and respect for client freedom. By dependably using the force of brain research, advertisers can lay out commonly gainful associations, lay areas of strength for out with the devotees they need to offer to, and make bargains.

1.2 Key Principles of Effective Sales Communication.

Viable deals correspondence is basic for creating incredible client connections and producing business development. It is the specialty of introducing messages and data to a crowd of people in a manner that enraptured them, addresses their requirements, and convinces them to act. Understanding and applying the essential ideas of compelling deals correspondence can significantly further develop your business viability and by and large achievement, whether you are a business expert, business visionary, or entrepreneur. We will take a gander at the basic thoughts that oversee viable deals in this article.

•Perceive Your Crowd

Understanding your crowd is one of the main parts of good deals correspondence. It is basic to get data about your expected clients, like their socioeconomics, inclinations, needs, and problem areas, prior to taking part in any deals discourse. With this understanding, you can customize your message and way to deal with their singular necessities and interests. By tailoring your communication to their particular circumstances, you can build trust and a relationship with them, increasing the likelihood of a successful sales outcome.

•Listening Effectively

Successful deal correspondence involves something other than conveying your message; it additionally involves undivided attention. Listening cautiously to your possibilities permits you to acquire valuable bits of knowledge, grasp their concerns, and pinpoint their fundamental inspirations. You lay out a positive compatibility and trust by showing certifiable consideration and sympathy. Your salespeople's credibility will grow as a result of your ability to effectively respond to their individual needs and concerns through active listening.

•Concision and lucidity

Lucidity and succinctness are fundamental in deal correspondence. Your message ought to be succinct, simple to get a handle on, and liberated from equivocalness. It is discouraged to make use of jargon or technical terms that could lead your readers astray. Make a short message that spotlights the fundamental issues and advantages that mean quite a bit to your possibilities. You might keep their consideration and forestall data over-burden by being brief.

•Enticing Language Use

Influence is fundamental in deal correspondence. Convincing language can help you in actually conveying the worth and advantages of your item or administration. Highlight the features and benefits of your service that will satisfy your customers' needs and appeal to them most. Furthermore, use narrating methodologies to sincerely draw in your crowd and make your message more recollected.

•Versatility

There is no one-size-fits-all strategy to deal with correspondence. It is basic to be versatile and alter your correspondence style in view of your possibilities' inclinations and correspondence designs. A more formal manner is preferred by some, while a conversational and more casual manner is preferred by others. You might establish an agreeable climate for your possibilities by being versatile, empowering better contribution and understanding.

•Making Trust.

Trust is the groundwork of good deals correspondence. Genuineness, straightforwardness, and uprightness help to assemble trust. In your contacts, be veritable and valid, conveying precise data and sensible assumptions regarding your item or administration. Offer no excessive expressions or vows that you can't keep. Trust is a fundamental structure block for long haul client connections and repeating business.

•The ability to understand people on a deeper level (EQ)

The capacity to distinguish and get a grip on one's own feelings along with comprehending the feelings of others is alluded to as the capacity to understand individuals on a deeper level. It is fundamental in deal correspondence since it empowers you to explore and answer really to the numerous profound states shown by your possibilities. You might interface with your crowd on a more profound level and really settle their concerns in the event that you show sympathy and understanding.

•Energy and certainty
Certainty and energy are infectious, and they can essentially affect the outcome of your deals correspondence. With confidence and knowledge of the value of your product or service, present yourself. Show your energy and enthusiasm for what you're giving, since this will move likely possibilities to share your excitement. At the point when you are energized and sure, your possibilities are bound to trust your ideas and go with a busy choice.

•Laying out Unambiguous Objectives
Laying out clear targets prior to taking part in any business communications is basic. Putting forth characterized objectives helps you to keep

on track and guide the correspondence's way. Having characterized targets assists you with coordinating your message and suggestions to take action proficiently, whether it's to make a deal, plan a gathering, or accumulate more data.

•Successful Cross examination

The capacity to pose legitimate inquiries is a basic part of good deals correspondence. With very much created requests, you might gain some significant experience about your possibilities' necessities, torment regions, and thought processes. Unassuming inquiries advance association and permit your possibilities to communicate their thoughts totally. You can change your correspondence to suit their singular requirements and give appropriate arrangements by listening cautiously to their reactions.

•Value proposition. An effective value proposition is necessary for effective sales communication. Obviously depict the particular worth and advantages that your item or administration gives. Stress how it tackles an issue, fills a need, or gives you an upper hand. Your worth deal ought to be brief, enticing, and zeroed in on the results and advantages that your possibilities can expect.

• **Overcoming Obstacles** .In sales, objections are inevitable. For successful sales communication, it is essential to respond to concerns in a manner that is appealing and professional. Rather than disregarding or contending with complaints, use them to get more data and resolve issues. Understanding the major reasons for complaints permits you to give fitting data or replies to alleviate any worries or reservations.

•**Relationship Building and Follow-up**
A solitary discussion doesn't comprise the finish of deals correspondence. Developing associations with possibilities and following them is basic for long haul achievement. Circle back to demands as quickly as time permits, give additional data, and answer any unanswered inquiries. Stay in contact on a regular basis to

remain top of mind and foster the relationship. You increment your possibilities bringing a deal to a close and getting rehash business by displaying your responsibility and steadfastness.

•Correspondence through Nonverbal Means
Compelling deals correspondence goes past the composed word. Non-verbal communication, facial motions, and manner of speaking are all nonverbal signs that impact how your message is seen. Be aware of your own nonverbal signals and ensure they match your ideal message. Focus on your possibilities' nonverbal pieces of information also, since they can uncover their degree of commitment and receptivity.

•Consistent Upgrade
Deals correspondence is an expertise that can be sharpened through time. Look for criticism consistently, audit your exhibition, and track down regions for development. Partake in deals instructional courses, read suitable books, and gain from successful salesman. Embrace a development mindset and attempt new

methodologies and systems to further develop your deals correspondence execution.

A vital part of fruitful deals tasks is compelling deals correspondence. You may significantly expand your capacity to draw in possibilities, make trust, and impact their buying choices by getting it and applying the primary standards referenced in this article. Make sure to customize your message to your crowd's prerequisites, to effectively tune in, to utilize convincing language, to change in accordance with correspondence inclinations, and to foster trust through genuineness and compassion. Constantly foster your abilities by tolerating remarks and making progress toward consistent improvement. You might build your deals achievement and foster long haul client connections by learning the ideas of good deals corresponding.

Chapter 2

Crafting Compelling Messages

Creating convincing messages is a fundamental ability in different parts of correspondence, going from business and showcasing to relational connections. A compelling message is one that not only piques the interest of the audience but also has a more profound impact on them. In this investigation, we will dig into the critical standards and procedures for creating messages that are convincing as well as noteworthy.

•Figuring out Your Crowd

The underpinning of a convincing message lies in a profound comprehension of the interest group. Prior to creating any message, it is critical to distinguish and investigate the socioeconomics, inclinations, and necessities of the crowd. This information permits communicators to tailor their messages to reverberate with the particular interests and worries of their crowd, making the correspondence more pertinent and locking in.

•Clearness and Succinctness

Successful correspondence requires lucidity and brevity. A convincing message ought to be clear in its goal and stay away from pointless intricacy. The message's impact can be diminished and confusion can result from ambiguity. On the other hand, conciseness ensures that the message can be understood by the audience and does not overburden them with unnecessary information. Quickness is in many cases key in catching and keeping up with consideration.

•Close to home Allure

Feeling assumes a strong part in shaping the human way of behaving. Engaging the audience's feelings is an essential part of crafting an engaging message. Whether it's satisfaction, dread, fervor, or sympathy, bringing out feelings makes an association and makes the message more essential. Utilizing engaging stories, individual tales, or genuinely charged language can assist with enhancing the profound allure of a message.

•Narrating Strategies

Stories have an exceptional capacity to enthrall a crowd of people. Integrating narrating procedures into messages can make them really captivating and appealing. A very much created story with a convincing plot, interesting characters, and a goal that reverberates with the crowd can have an enduring effect. Not only does telling a story get people's attention, but it also helps people understand and remember more difficult concepts.

• **Establishing Credibility.**In order to be persuasive, a compelling message must establish credibility. This includes introducing realities, insights, or tributes that help the central issues of the message. Individuals are bound to trust and be convinced by messages that come from a sound source. Since authenticity is a crucial component of effective communication, being transparent and honest is another aspect of credibility building.

•Source of inspiration

A convincing message ought to incite the crowd to make a move. Whether it's making a buy, buying into a help, or changing a way of behaving, it is reasonable and it is fundamental to force a source of inspiration. The call to action ought to be precise, attainable, and in line with the message as a whole. Making a need to keep moving or offering motivators can additionally inspire the crowd to instantly act.

•Visual Allure

In the computerized age, visual components assume a huge part in correspondence. Integrating outwardly engaging parts, like pictures, infographics, or recordings, can upgrade the general effect of a message. Visuals not only help get people's attention, but they also make it easier to convey complicated information. The utilization of variety, typography, and plan components ought to line up with the expected message and the inclinations of the interest group.

•Consistency Across Stages

In the present interconnected world, messages frequently range across different stages and channels. Building a coherent and recognizable brand necessitates maintaining messaging consistency across all media. Consistency supports the message and reinforces the general effect on the crowd. Whether it's a web-based entertainment post, email, or a show, keeping a brought together message adds to a seriously convincing and critical correspondence system.

•Versatility and Adaptability

Viable communicators figure out the significance of versatility. Based on the changing requirements and preferences of the audience, messages might need to be modified. Adaptability in adjusting the tone, style, and content of a message guarantees that it stays significant and thunderous. Observing criticism and remaining sensitive to changes in the outside climate permits communicators to make convenient changes for most extreme effect.

•Testing and Cycle

Making convincing messages is an iterative interaction. Testing different message varieties and examining their adequacy is fundamental for refining and streamlining correspondence systems. A/B testing, reviews, and criticism systems furnish important experiences into what reverberates with the crowd. By persistently refining messages in view of information and criticism, communicators can improve the general effect and viability of their correspondence endeavors.

Creating convincing messages is both a workmanship and a science. It requires a profound comprehension of the crowd, successful narrating, close to home reverberation, and an essential way to deal with correspondence channels. By zeroing in on lucidity, profound allure, believability, and a solid source of inspiration, communicators can make messages that catch consideration as well as drive significant commitment. In a consistently developing correspondence scene, the capacity to create convincing messages is a significant expertise that rises above businesses and settings, making it a foundation of effective correspondence systems.

2.1 Identifying Customer Pain Points and Desires .

Individuals have an inborn skeptical tendency, meaning we will by and large enlist critical updates even more instantly and harp on those experiences all the more consistently. A comparative quirk applies to clients and their pain points

Notwithstanding the way that it is basic to examine all of the benefits and surprising components of your thing, clients will undoubtedly push toward a purchase decision expecting that they feel your thing can moderate the disquiet of their consistent pain points.

By recognizing and watching out for client pain points in your advancing and bargain tries, you can concoct a truly persuading philosophy that will make your association significant as per your clients.

• Where are the problems?

Trouble spots are persistent issues with a product or service that can be problematic for customers and their businesses. Then again to simply put it, they're dismissed necessities fit to be satisfied.

Client anguish can be associated with their own or capable resides and can be physical, up close and personal, or vital.

A couple of potential outcomes may not realize the pain points they are experiencing. You should convince them that they have a problem and that your organization has a solution.

•Guidelines to Perceive Client Pain points

We understand that pain points are issues that clients and potential outcomes experience, yet how might you recognize them?

Pain points can be essentially as varied and unique as people who experience them, so it makes a big difference to guide emotional investigation to uncover the possibility of your client's problem areas. Truly around then could you anytime fathom where you fit in to fix them.

Here are some steps that can be taken to locate those trouble spots.

•Attract with clients.

The best method for finding your client's pain points is to permit them to clearly tell you. Lead client research, for instance, studies, focus social affairs, and gatherings.

By presenting assigned requests and listening enthusiastically to client responses, you might even more at any point probably understand and handle their interests. You should similarly do live visits on your site so clients and conceivable outcomes can contact you with questions and issues.

•Ask your bunch.

Your association's effort bunch converses with conceivable outcomes and clients reliably. They're a huge wellspring of information on your clients' consistent pain points and how you can push ahead to settle them.

Your effort gathering will in like manner have a substitute perspective on client pain points that can help you with finding stowed examples and even trouble spots dark to specific clients.

In any case, you should be careful to promise you are isolating between client pain points and pain points your effort gathering may be experiencing, accepting that they are encountering issues closing deals.

• Examine customer feedback.

Your clients and potential clients are sensibly coursing out their pain points on the web. Accepting you know where to look, you can change those areas of burden areas of strength into centers for your business.

Take apart your client administration passes to learn about your clients' pain points, and tune in up through electronic amusement and online studies to find out where people in your industry are feeling torture. Consider social listening programming to help with this task.

•Pain point Models

We'll isolate more unambiguous circumstances further in this article, but most importantly, coming up next are two or three general sorts of pain points you could go over.

A client requires assistance with their spending plan. Money related limits keep clients from working beneficially and lead them to search for extra adroit choices.

A business with an exorbitant number of monotonous steps in its technique. An overabundance of cycle lead time costs money and uncovers a need to diminish it.

inconsistent communication between divisions. Bunches need to sort out some way to bestow information suitably to at the same time lessen botches.

These are conditions that cause "desolation" or cover productivity. The most imperative stage in addressing these desolations is knowing how to recognize and kill them, so we ought to discuss how to do it for your clients.

2.2 Developing a Unique Value Proposition

In second's very serious business world, undertakings that need to stand apart from the group and draw in target visitors should make a novel offer(UVP). A novel incentive(UVP) is a concise explanation that stresses the particular advantages, worth, and confinement that an item or administration gives to its visitors. It's a significant device for imparting a brand's unity, tending to purchaser issues, or satisfying client requests in manners that challengers can not. In this creation, we will take a gander at how to deliver a drawing in UVP and present epitomes to show its importance.

Understanding the Secerning Incentive.

An UVP ought to make sense of what recognizes an organization or item and why visitors ought to pick it over challengers. To deliver a viable UVP, an itemized comprehension of the objective solicitation, serious geology, and client needs and inclinations is required. The subsequent steps are crucial to the creation of a charming UVP.

•**Decide your objective solicitation** Understanding your objective followership's necessities, articles, and torment regions is basic. Direct solicitation investigation, checks, and client meetings to realize what your certain visitors need and how your item or administration might satisfy their needs. analyze the opposition By measuring the serious landscape, you can track down holes and opportunities for detachment. Understanding what challengers offer permits you to accentuate exceptional highlights or advantages that recognize your immolation.

• **Define your unique selling proposition (USP).** An essential component of your UVP is your USP. It alludes to the unmistakable mark of your item or administration that sets it piecemeal from the opposition. This could be a point, an innovation edge, remarkable client administration, or an imaginative way to deal with issue goals. produce an unmistakable and brief explanation that makes sense of the worth your item or administration gives to visitors. Focus on the advantages and issues that visitors can expect assuming they pick your outcome. Make sure your UVP is accessible to your target audience and steer clear of specialized slang.

•**Test and redesign**

In the wake of making a first UVP, put it under a magnifying glass with your objective followership.

Request criticism and make variations grounded on it. A UVP ought to be a living document that evolves in response to customer requests and requests. Powerful Exceptional Offer representations

Apple "Assume Unique" Apple's UVP centers around creation, straightforwardness, and stoner-altruism. Apple has secured itself as an innovation assiduity pioneer by challenging the current quo and immolation items that are natural and stylishly lovely.

" Have a place Anyplace" with Airbnb. Airbnb's UVP underscores its ability to deliver stand-out and customized trip visitors . Airbnb permits buyers to drench themselves in unique social orders by connecting them with unique has and outfitting a decision of lodgment , making a feeling of having a place that customary hospices can not give.

"Speeding up the World's Change to Reasonable Energy," Tesla claims. Tesla's UVP spins around the organization's obligation to supportable energy results. By developing high-performing electric vehicles and promoting sustainable energy technology, Tesla has deposed itself as a colonial machine manufacturer, appealing to environmentally conscious customers.

Bone Shave Club's watchword is" Shave Time. Shave magnates.

" The UVP of Dollar Shave Club is convenience and sensibility. They give visitors with a practical and bother free volition to customary retail choices by offering a membership grounded approach for razors and fixing specifics.

The slogan for Zappos is "Delivering Happiness." Great customer service is Zappos's unique selling point. Zappos has recognized itself in the serious web-based retail industry by focusing on client joy and giving free delivery and returns, acting in purchaser loyalty and verbal exchange references.

Determination, Making a particular worth proposition is basic for endeavors looking to hang out at the time's cutthroat landscape. A switching UVP helps attract guests and keep them coming back by highlighting the uniqueness and value of a product or service. By investigating the needs of the target audience, evaluating the competition, defining distinctive selling propositions, and effectively communicating value, businesses can cultivate a connection with their customer base. The examples provided demonstrate how success and customer fidelity are affected by a well-written UVP. Streak back that an UVP ought to develop in light of changing solicitation conditions and client possibilities to guarantee that the brand stays relevant and cutthroat.

Chapter 3

Mastering Storytelling

For a very long time, storytelling has been an important part of human culture. It can captivate, attract, and inspire swarms. Narrating has arisen as a strong showcasing and deals device lately. Companies can improve brand awareness, make a stronger connection with their customers, and ultimately drive deals by incorporating narrative strategies into deal pitches and introductions.

•Characters that are engaging

Characters are the substance of a story. Characters who are progressed and intriguing let the group associate earnestly with the story. In a professional workplace, these characters could be customers, employees, or even the actual brand.

• **Close to home Relativity Profound stories are bound to resound.** Associations could propel compassion, spread out trust, and make a fundamental experience that connection points with their vested party by drawing in their sentiments.

•Realness is central for uncommon describing

Associations should endeavor to convey trustworthy stories that are solid with their characteristics, mission, and brand character. Validness increases credibility and spreads out a more grounded relationship with the group.

Business Describing Appreciates Many Advantages

•Making Serious solid areas for a Character

Organizations can make an unmistakable brand personality that separates them from contenders by integrating stories into their image technique. Important stories assist with people's structure insights, structure profound associations, and build up the upsides of a brand.

•**Drawing in Clients.** Narrating is an extraordinary way for organizations to interface with their clients on a close to home level. Associations could spread out a sensation of trustworthiness and long stretch purchaser responsibility by letting stories in on that resonate with their vested party.

•**Association Vision Correspondence**
Stories are areas of strength for conferring an association's vision, mission, and goals. Associations can rouse and engage laborers by presenting these thoughts in story structure, delivering a typical ability to know east from west and heading.

• **Impact of Partners.** Whether financial backers, accomplices, or the overall population are involved, story can possibly be a powerful instrument for convincing partners. Accounts that are particularly made may show the value recommendation, collect support, and drive needed results.

Overwhelming Business Describing Strategies:

•**Decide Your Essential Message.** Prior to developing a narrative, organizations should determine their essential message. The message should be clear, short, and as per the targets of the describing project.

• **Recognize the potential origins of members of Your Audience**
Realizing your vested party is major for interfacing with the story. In order to tailor the narrative to the intended audience, organizations ought to assess their socioeconomic status, interests, and thought processes.

•**Use Unmistakable Language and Imagery**
To manufacture mental pictures in the characters of the group, associating with describing relies upon clear language and imagery. The story has a more personal impact when expressive language and tactile data are used.

•**Coordinate Battle and Objective.**Battle is a huge piece of describing in light of the fact that it produces strain and prompts the story forward. Associations could show their ability to beat burden and element their value proposition by presenting troubles and obstructions.

•**Utilize Genuine Models.** Tales and genuine models can make a business story all the more genuine and interesting. Associations could make their accounts truly enchanting and viable by including helpful experiences.

Grasping the key standards, advantages, and approaches of compelling narrating is the most important move toward dominating narrating in business. Storylines can be utilized by organizations to fabricate areas of strength for a character, get clients genuinely involved, make sense of their main goal, and impact partners. In the current relentless scene, when abilities to concentrate are short, succeeding at business describing is a key capacity that can isolate an association, cultivate affiliations, and drive accomplishment.

3.1 Impact of Storytelling in Sales

Storytelling has been an integral part of human civilization for thousands of years. It is capable of captivating, inspiring, and engaging viewers. Narrative has become a powerful sales and marketing strategy in recent years. By incorporating storytelling techniques into sales pitches and presentations, businesses may be able to strengthen connections with their clients, raise awareness of their brands, and ultimately increase sales. This article analyzes the strong effect of account in deals, underscoring its benefits and introducing certifiable instances of its prosperity.

- **Emotional Connections.**Storytelling makes it possible for salespeople to emotionally connect with their target audience. A very much created story, as opposed to shooting them with information and figures, invigorates feelings and advances sympathy. Salesmen can make sense of the worth of their item or administration in a thoughtful and critical manner by sharing individual stories, tales, or contextual investigations. A sales rep showcasing a wellbeing and wellness application, for instance, could see a story of a client application to modify their life, featuring the profound excursion and the great impact it had on their prosperity.

• **Overcoming Objections and Resistance.**In sales, potential customers' objections and resistance are frequent roadblocks. Narrating can be a powerful methodology for conquering these snags. By telling stories of past customers who initially had reservations or concerns but ultimately found success with the product or service, sales professionals can calm fears and boost confidence. These tales act as friendly confirmation, demonstrating that others have had gainful results and expanding the contribution's authenticity.

•Distinguishing Yourself from Your Competitors. It might be hard to stand out in a crowded market. The art of storytelling offers a one-of-a-kind chance to set a product or service apart from the competition. Deals experts can foster a particular character that reverberates with clients by creating a convincing story around the brand's set of experiences, convictions, or mission. For instance, a sales rep for a supportable dress business could recount the tale of how the firm was framed determined to decrease the natural impact of the design business, hence interesting to biologically delicate purchasers.

•Enhancing Memorability. Humans are hardwired to remember stories rather than a long list of features or advantages. At the point when you integrate narrating into your attempts to sell something, you make the substance more recalled and significant. Deals experts might make their information really intriguing and less difficult to recollect by giving realities and information inside a story structure. A salesman selling a network safety arrangement, for instance, could see a story about an organization that was the casualty of a digital attack, underlining the outcomes and stressing how their item might have stayed away from it.

•Establishing a Drawn out Connection

Effective deals include something beyond a one-time exchange; they try to lay out long haul associations. Narrating adds to the formation of an enduring impression that reaches out past the underlying exchange. Deals experts can make faithfulness and support rehash business by conveying stories that resound with the client's qualities, goals, or issues. For instance, a sales rep selling instructive programming could see examples of overcoming adversity of understudies who utilized the program to make scholarly progress, laying out an enduring impression of the worth it adds to their schooling.

Conclusion,Storytelling has been created as an intense deals system, furnishing a way to interface with clients, beat protests, separate from contenders, further develop memorability, and have an enduring impression. Using the power of narrative, sales professionals can transform their pitches into memorable experiences that connect with customers on an emotional level. By integrating narration into the deals interaction, associations can fortify their connections, raise brand mindfulness, and at last lift deals. In a data over-burden world, narrating is an immortal and strong strategy for enthralling the hearts and psyches of clients.

3.2 Choosing the Right Stories for Effect

In the domain of arrangements, the ability to get the thought and attract the sensations of potential clients is pressing. One in number strategy for achieving this is through describing. Stories have the phenomenal ability to connect with individuals on a significant level, helping them with interfacing with your thing or organization and finally influencing their purchasing decisions. Nevertheless, not all records are made the same, and picking the right stories for most prominent effect in bargains requires cognizant ideas. In this article, we'll look at the most important factors to keep in mind when choosing stories that will captivate your audience and close deals.

•Identify Your Target Audience. Having a thorough understanding of your target audience is crucial when selecting stories for deals. Put away an edge to explore and break down your clients' economics, psychographics, and pain points. You will be able to select stories that resonate with their experiences, needs, and desires with the help of this information. By accommodating your records to your group, you increase the conceivable outcomes of making a genuine affiliation and getting the best significant response.

•Change Stories to Your Picture
While picking stories for gives, it is principal to ensure they line up with your picture character and values. The most important messages you

need to convey about your product or service should be supported by your account. Contemplate the tone, style, and subjects of your picture and pick stories that enhance and sustain your general picture account. This consistency will establish areas of strength for a central connection, further developing your clients' endlessly trust in your commitments.

•Highlight Benefits and Courses of action

The records you pick should pressure the benefits and courses of action your thing or organization gives. People are by and large determined by moral obligation, searching for deals with their interests or needs. Create narratives that demonstrate the change you have brought about and the outcomes you have achieved, emphasizing the significance of your contributions for other people. By focusing on the value and results, you make your records significant and persuasive to anticipated clients, influencing their dynamic cycle.

•Use Client Instances of defeating affliction

Perhaps the most exceptional kind of story in bargains is the client's instance of defeating affliction. It can be very powerful to share real examples of how your product or service has solved problems or helped customers. These accounts provide social validation by demonstrating that other people have achieved success and enabling expected customers to imagine themselves in similar circumstances. Client instances of conquering difficulty can be shared through recognitions, context oriented examinations, or even video interviews, adding authenticity and legitimacy to your endeavor to sell something.

•Impact Significant Triggers

Sentiments expect a basic part of course, and coordinating up close and personal triggers into your records can essentially overhaul their impact. Consider the sentiments you want to gather in your group, similar to elation, fear, or sympathy, and select stories that resound with those sentiments. For example, a story that makes the most of the sensation of fear toward missing a significant open door or the yearning for mindfulness can be significantly powerful. By interfacing with the sensations of your group, you make a central and compelling experience that sits tight for them long after the arrangement's collaboration.

•Make a Story Curve

A particularly made story follows a record twist, taking the group on an outing from battle to objective. While picking stories for bargains, ensure they have a sensible development that gets thought, manufactures strain, and finally gives a phenomenal objective. This structure withstands dedication and has a long-lasting effect. Consider solidifying parts like a drawing in legend, a persuading conflict, and an objective that includes the value of your thing or organization.

•Keep Stories Brief and Significant

In bargains, time is generally speaking confined, and capacities to concentrate can be short.

Therefore, it is essential to select stories that are brief and pertinent to the particular circumstance. Avoid broad records or diversions that could redirect or break your group down. In light of everything, revolve around the middle parts of the story that directly support your arrangement's message. You can keep up with the audience's interest and increase the impact of your narration by telling stories that are engaging, succinct, and directly relevant to the discussion about the deals.

•Incorporate Grouping

While it's fundamental to stay aware of consistency and change your records to your picture, solidifying arrangement in your describing approach can be helpful. Different clients have different tendencies and answer different describing styles. Consider using a mix of individual stories, client instances of conquering difficulty, industry context oriented examinations, and, shockingly, made up stories to deal with different inclinations and interface with a greater extent of potential clients. This assortment keeps your plans introductions new and guarantees that you can change your depiction to various circumstances and people.

• **Test and Improve.**Selecting the best stories for deals is an iterative process. It's fundamental to ceaselessly test and refine your depicting approach thinking about examination and results. Base on the responses and obligation levels of your gathering during deals introductions. Collect contributions from your work, social events and clients to get a handle on which stories are resounding and which could require improvement. Utilize A/B testing and evaluation to correspondingly gauge the reasonableness of various stories and change your system. By reliably refining your depicting structure, you can develop its effect and determinedly further cultivate your plans execution.

• **Practice and Movement** .It goes without saying that even the most persuasive story can fail spectacularly if it is not conveyed honestly.

After selecting the appropriate stories for deals, concentrate on practicing and admiring your vehicle. Base on your tone, pacing, non-verbal correspondence, and in ordinary show limits. Work on relating your records with confirmation, energy, and realness. To improve the impact of your portrayal, ponder consolidating blended media components like pictures or props. Keep in mind, what you convey your records can essentially mean for their practicality in getting thought and animating development.

It takes cautious thought and information on your interest group, brand, and wanted results to choose the best stories for the best effect in bargains. By changing your records to your gathering's necessities and needs, featuring the advantages and courses of action of your responsibilities, utilizing critical triggers, and joining client occasions of overcoming disaster, you can make convincing stories that draw in possible clients and drive deals. Try to keep your records brief, basic, and remarkable, while perseveringly testing, refining, and further cultivating your depicting approach. Your records will become helpful resources in your arrangements with enduring impressions and solid impact on buying choices with preparing and convincing conveyance.

Without a doubt, even the most persuasive story can fail spectacularly if it isn't conveyed truly. At the point when you have picked the right stories for bargains, focus on practicing and admiring your transport. Center around your tone, pacing, non-verbal correspondence, and in everyday show capacities. Work on relating your records with assurance, energy, and realness. To enhance the effect of your narration, think about incorporating mixed media elements like images or props. Remember, how you convey your records can basically affect their feasibility in getting thought and rousing movement.

It takes careful consideration and knowledge of your target audience, brand, and desired outcomes to select the best stories for the greatest impact in deals. By changing your records to your group's necessities and wants, highlighting the benefits and game plans of your commitments, using significant triggers, and combining client instances of conquering misfortune, you can make persuading stories that attract potential clients and drive bargains. Make a point to keep your records brief, critical, and unique, while relentlessly testing, refining, and further fostering your describing approach. Your accounts will become useful assets in your deals stockpile with lasting impressions and strong influence on purchasing decisions with training and compelling delivery.

Chapter 4

Effective Communication Skills

In the business region, strong correspondence divides are key. They spread out the root serious areas of strength for, support, and driving business accomplishment. Experts need to be able to communicate effectively in all situations, whether it's to share ideas with coworkers, bargain with visitors, or give gifts to partners. This paper takes a gander at the main parts of successful correspondence and gives true guides to show how they work in a business setting.

• Unimaginably Clear and Minimized Language Convincing business correspondence requires the use of clear and brief language. Utilizing exact language to pass on thoughts, directions, or data decreases confusion and increases appreciation. It's furthermore essential to avoid work related chatter or explicit explanations that may be surprising to all social occasions included. outline, An arrangement boss uses careful and brief language to bestow the compass, things, and dates of one more arrangement during a unit meeting. Partners could comprehend the arrangement conditions essentially and truly by diminishing delicate comprehensive articulations down into direct language and avoiding specific business related chatter.

•Harkening strenuously

Full focus is a critical part of good correspondence. It includes focusing on both verbal and nonverbal signs, showing real interest, and arduously harkening back to the speaker. Individuals who persevere can see the value in the contemplations of others, handle tries, and design more grounded bonds. An arrangements director, for example, cautiously pays attention to the client's requirements in a client meeting, giving specific consideration to their tone, non-verbal communication, and concerns. The association shows their steadiness to understanding and meeting the client's prospects by surrendering the client's necessities and asking material ensuing requests.

•The capacity to comprehend individuals at their center and Compassion. Sympathy and the ability to see the value in people on a more profound level are central for strong correspondence. Understanding and interfacing with the impressions of people enables specialists to make trust, spread out affiliation, and orchestrate delicate addresses with class. Compassion adds to the development of a scene in which people feel appreciated, appreciated, and understood. In a presentation overview, for portrayal, a central character shows compassion by fitting a hand's difficulties and conveying formative talk in a strong manner. By feting the hand's sweat and furnishing thoughts for development, the main cultivates a friendly and accommodating domain that asks the individual to create and make.

•Correspondence that isn't verbal

In business exchanges, verbal correspondence like looks, movements, and non-verbal correspondence can shoot huge dispatches. Understanding and using verbal thoughts appropriately can work on the general impact and clearness of correspondence. Staying in contact, using open and inviting non-verbal correspondence, and checking imaginative conflicts in verbal correspondence are vital. A smart go-between, for depiction, stays in contact with the counterparty, slants forward to show thought, and uses sensible hand signs to stress major concentrations during a business concession. The middle person makes trust and legitimacy by using positive verbal thoughts, which adds to a viable objective.

•Design and clearness in composed Correspondence, similar to gifts, messages, and reports, is a fundamental part of business associations. Writing that is very clear and well-organized aids in the effective transmission of information, reduces confusion, and safeguards a professional image. Strong formed correspondence requires rehearsing extraordinary letter sets, putting together things reasonably, and getting on with the asked correspondence. portrayal, A displaying master makes a magnificent dispatch to comprehended guests that really approaches the upsides of another thing and consolidates a wellspring of motivation. By utilizing succinct language, actually putting together the message, and editing for lucidity, the master improves the probability of connecting with the givers and creating great reactions.

•Discourse And Developmental Survey

Giving feedback and participating in a developmental survey are essential components of productive business correspondence. Specialists could help their accomplices and separation people create and work on their show by equipping clear, valuable info. Developmental assessment ought to be given in a circumspect way a positive supporting and an emphasis on the gest or activity as opposed to the existent. A unit boss, for frame, may hold an analysis meeting with an organization part, pressing their resources and locales for update. By outfitting specific embodiments, developing ideas for progress, and emphasizing the unit component's potential, the pioneer provides a setting that encourages professional events and cultivates a culture of continuous improvement.

4.1 Active Listening and Empathy

Full focus and compassion are two key capacities for bargain reasonability. They help you with sorting out your conceivable outcomes' necessities, challenges, and sentiments, and make a decent affiliation that structures similarity and trust. In this article, you will sort out some way to use full focus and empathy to additionally foster your business conversations and results.

What is full focus?

Full focus is the demonstration of giving full thought to what your chance is referring to, without encroaching, judging, or redirecting yourself. It incorporates using verbal and non-verbal prompts to show that you are tuning in, such as signaling, smiling, and revamping. Full focus in like manner suggests presenting genuine requests, making sense of centers, and summarizing key messages.

What is empathy?

Compassion is the ability to pause for a moment to think about your chance's viewpoint and handle their opinions, thoughts, and perspectives. It isn't comparable to empathy, which is having a baffled outlook on someone. Compassion is connected to showing genuine interest and care, and perceiving your chance's sentiments. Compassion helps you with building fondness and trust, as well as uncover hidden necessities and fights.

The best technique to include full focus and empathy in bargains

Full focus and compassion are methods, yet mindsets that you need to take on in each arrangement conversation. To use them, as a matter of fact, arranging mentally before the call, setting a positive point and getting your mind liberated from interruptions is huge. Listen more than you talk and use smart clarifications, for instance, expressions that reflect what your chance has said, to show that you are tuning in and understanding. Ask probing questions to get more information, refute complaints, and dispel suspicions. Endorse your chance's sentiments to create trust and similarity, and express compassion and backing to make a decent up close and personal affiliation. Doing so will show that you are a salesperson, but an associate.

How full focus and empathy benefit your arrangements

Using full focus and empathy can vehemently influence your business execution and results. You can better understand their needs and design your pitch by developing compatibility and trust with them. This can make them more open to your ideas. In addition, showing these capacities can isolate you from competitors and augmentation buyer steadfastness, relentlessly, and references. As a result, you'll be more likely to engage in repetitive business and positive verbal exchanges. The best way to reduce your capacity for compassion and full concentration is to seek advice from potential outcomes, partners, and executives. Check your business calls to see where things are pushing ahead. Obtain different game plans, trained professionals and read books, articles, and destinations concerning the matter. Additionally, put these abilities to utilize consistently to make them more normal and compelling.

Concentration and compassion are strong resources that can fundamentally affect the progress of an arrangement. Bargain specialists can fabricate similarity, lay out trust, and improve the probability of finalizing a negotiation by successfully captivating clients, figuring out their necessities, and answering truly. In addition, by feeling for clients, figuring out their opinions, and fitting answers for their particular necessities, agents can make traversing affiliations, support resolute quality, and make go over business.

4.2 Overcoming Objections and Building Rapport

In the cutthroat universe of deals, beating complaints and building compatibility are basic abilities that can represent the moment of truth and arrangement. Protests from potential clients are unavoidable, yet they ought not be viewed as barricades. All things considered, deal experts ought to see complaints as any open doors to draw in with possibilities, address their interests, and eventually construct solid connections. This article investigates compelling methodologies for defeating protests and building compatibility in deals, empowering salesmen to close more arrangements and make more prominent progress.

Figuring out Complaints

Perceiving the Various Sorts of Complaints

Item related protests: These complaints emerge when possibilities have worries about the elements, quality, or reasonableness of the item or administration being advertised.

Concerns about prices: Clients might communicate complaints connected with the expense or an incentive for cash.

Timing protests: A possibility might defer their choice because of variables like financial plan imperatives or forthcoming tasks.

Authority protests: When the decision-maker is absent, these objections result in a lack of commitment.

Undivided attention and Sympathy
Listening mindfully permits salesmen to completely figure out the possibility's interests and protests.

Compassion assists experts with connecting with the possibility's viewpoint, exhibiting that they comprehend and think often about their necessities.

•Expect and Plan

Completely research the item, market, and ideal interest group to expect possible complaints.

Foster all around contemplated reactions to normal complaints, giving enticing contentions and proof to address each worry.

Answering Successfully

Recognize the protest: Show appreciation for the possibility's feedback and approve their interests.

Explain the protest: Pose unconditional inquiries to acquire a more profound comprehension of the protest.

•Give a custom-made reaction: Address the complaint explicitly, featuring the advantages and interesting incentive of the item or administration.

•**Utilize social evidence**: To instill confidence in the prospect, share customer success stories or testimonials.

•**Offer other options:** Assuming the protest is certified, investigate elective arrangements that might better address the possibility's issues. Transform Protests into Open doors

•**Reevaluate complaints as questions.**Urge the possibility to consider issues with a chance to dive deeper into the item or administration.

•**Instruct and illuminate:** Use protests as an opportunity to give extra data that explains misinterpretations or dissipates questions.

•**Use complaint dealing as a method for building compatibility**: Salespeople build trust with prospects and demonstrate their expertise by effectively responding to objections.
•**Establishing Trust**: Be sincere and authentic in your interactions.

Show skill and industry information to impart trust in your possibilities.

Show honesty by completely finishing responsibilities and commitments.

Active Communication To comprehend the preferences and requirements of the prospect, employ active listening skills.

To open up conversation and find out more information, ask pertinent questions.

Tailor your correspondence style to match the possibility's inclinations, adjusting your way to deal with fabricating an association.

To establish a sense of familiarity, look for shared interests or experiences.

Feature any common associations or affiliations to fabricate affinity and trust.

Personalize the Experience. Keep the prospect's name in mind and use it in conversations.

Make an effort to comprehend their particular challenges and objectives, and then adapt your strategy accordingly.

To demonstrate ongoing support, follow up with personalized messages or recommendations.

In the realm of deals, beating complaints and building compatibility are essential parts of making progress. Salespeople can turn objections into opportunities and address potential customers' concerns by comprehending the various types of objections, actively listening to prospects, and effectively responding. It is significant to expect complaints, plan influential reactions, and give custom fitted arrangements that feature the worth of the item or administration. Also, building affinity through trust, dynamic correspondence, figuring out some mutual interest, and personalization is fundamental for laying areas of strength out with possibilities. By dominating these procedures, deals experts can explore complaints with certainty, construct compatibility with clients, and at last close more arrangements. Keep in mind, protests ought to be seen as venturing stones as opposed to hindrances, prompting further developed deals execution and long haul progress in the cutthroat deals scene.

Chapter 5

Negotiation and Closing Deals

Bargains experts who wish to close complex arrangements with bright partners, leaders, and dissuasions should be reasonable to arrange. This structure will teach you some fruitful concession techniques for prostrating bargain obstruction, making worth, and raising trust with your possibilities.

•Decide the significant players

Prior to going into a concession, you ought to comprehend who you are managing and what their liabilities, interests, and trouble spots are. test the business, the assiduity, and individuals took part in the dynamic cycle. Figure out who has the power, impact, and financial plan to approve the deal. Figure out who your verifiable abettors , enemies, or doorkeepers are and the way in which you may actually associate with them.

•Make your BATNA

BATNA is an abbreviation that represents snappy volition to an arranged understanding. In any case, this is your beautiful volition, In the event that the concession fizzles or hits an impasse. Realizing your BATNA can help you in setting sensible possibilities, staying away from unfriendly circumstances, and reinforcing your logrolling position. In order to prepare your BATNA, you must examine your druthers, estimate their value, and compare them to the proposed agreement.

•Figure association and trust

concession includes insights and rationale, yet in addition sentiments and relational relations. You should deliver association and entrust with your possibilities to change over them. You can work around this by paying close attention, harping patiently, asking open-ended questions, and communicating effectively with your body language. You should likewise exhibit your personality, experience, and offer, as well as show how your outcome can break their concerns and meet their circumstances.

•**Answer tests and questions**.

Dissuasions and inquiries are vital in any concession, especially in complex arrangements. They can show your possibilities' advantage, interest, or reluctance. You should move toward them with certainty, lucidity, and regard. To answer to dissuasions and requests, get the LAER model here, concede, test, and determine. hear to understand their ventures, appreciate their feelings, test the reasons and effects, and fix the issue with proof, embodiments, or witnesses.

Relying upon the conditions, you might have to utilize an assortment of concession styles to arrive at your asked outcome. A helpful procedure centers around aggregate interests, esteem, age, and long haul participation to accomplish a palm result that benefits the two players and supports the relationship. A cutthroat system involves seeking after a palm-lose result that expands your own advantages while limiting

5.1 Negotiation Dynamics and Strategies

The thoughts, techniques, and ways utilized to deliver commonly beneficial issues in bargain addresses are related to as concession elements and methodologies in bargains. Understanding the mechanics of the arranging system, practicing powerful styles, and utilizing beautiful strategies to boost the worth of the arrangements while keeping an ideal relationship with the client are all important for the cycle. Then, at that point, are a few significant qualities of arrangements concession elements and methodologies

•**Planning** **Exhaustive**.prescription is fundamental for fruitful facilities. This incorporates testing the client, figuring out their circumstances and interests, knowing your item or administration, and laying out clear concession objects.

•**Laying out Compatibility**.Laying out an ideal relationship and partnership with the client is basic. This can be satisfied by mindfully harkening, exhibiting compassion, and looking for a shared view. Building partnership advances participation and raises the responsibility of a palm outgrowth.

•Production of Significant worth Effective facilities focus on outfitting an incentive for the two players included. This can be satisfied through finding areas of aggregate interest, investigating new outcomes, and advancing your item's or alternately administration's advantages and special incentives.

•Unbending nature and Rigidity Facilities continually incorporate compromise. Being versatile and adaptable assists you with changing your arrangement, testing various outcomes, and arriving at arrangements that fulfill the two sides. It's basic to keep a receptive outlook and be anxious to attempt new impacts.

•**Successful Correspondence in bargain**.facilities, clear and decisive correspondence is fundamental. Utilize fulfilling contentions and validation to convey the worth and advantages of your immolation without any problem. Verbal signals, like non-verbal communication and manner of speaking, can likewise be utilized to communicate certainty and validity in powerful correspondence.

•Overseeing dissuasions in facilities, dissuasions are normal. Expect implied dissuasions and be prepared to answer with all around permitted

- our reactions. Address dissuasions with compassion, offer outcomes, and complement the worth of your item or administration.

•**Mutual benefit results**.Take a stab at palm issues in which the two players feel they've served. This methodology grows long haul hookups and raises the possibilities of unborn cooperation and repeat business.

•**Concession Strategies**. concession strategies remember outlining the conversation for terms of advantages as opposed to costs, outfitting numerous choices to give firmness, utilizing time-grounded motivations or restricted time offers, and utilizing correspondence by offering concessions in return for concessions from the other party.

Generally, bargain concession elements and styles incorporate a mix of drugs, compelling correspondence, relationship-structure, and an emphasis on creating an incentive for the two players. Bargains experts can improve their possibilities arriving at powerful issues in facilities by implementing these styles.

5.2 Effective Communication Techniques

Fruitful deals rely intensely upon compelling correspondence. To bring deals to a close and make persevering through client associations, it is fundamental to have the ability to convey thoughts, lay out compatibility, and convince others. The various communication techniques that salespeople can employ to improve their efficiency during the sales process will be examined in this article. To demonstrate the way that these strategies can be utilized in practical circumstances, we will analyze fundamental procedures that are upheld by models from certifiable circumstances. Sales reps can conquer obstructions, fabricate connections, and ultimately arrive at their deals targets by being proficient at these correspondence capacities.

•Dynamic Hearing

Successful correspondence in deals begins with undivided attention. It involves giving close consideration to what the purchaser is talking about, appreciating their needs, and actually responding. Salesmen can assemble affinity, track down significant data, and effectively address client worries by utilizing undivided attention strategies. For example, summing up and rewording what the shopper has said could show commitment while guaranteeing legitimate understanding. To show interest and consideration, undivided attention additionally involves nonverbal signs like keeping eye to eye connection and utilizing open non-verbal communication.

An illustration of this would be a salesperson conversing with a potential customer who is worried about the product's dependability. The salesperson actively listens, notes, and paraphrases the customer's concerns to demonstrate that they understand them. To promise the client that their interests have been recognized and thought about, they respond by underlining the extensive quality control systems set up.

•making a compatibility

As it advances trust and sets the connection between the sales rep and the client, creating compatibility is fundamental in deals. Interfacing with potential clients assists with laying out an inviting climate where they feel appreciated and comprehended. Tracking down marks of understanding, utilizing classy humor, and showing a genuine interest in the client's objectives and issues are great ways of creating compatibility.

For example, a sales rep could see an outlined photo of a games group in a possibility's working environment during a deals meeting. They start a conversation about sports to lay out compatibility and find shared belief. The climate is improved by this association, which works with a better conversation of the deals recommendation.

•Persuasive Communication. The objective of persuasive communication is to influence the customer's decision-making process positively by providing compelling facts. Salesmen can utilize different systems, including narrating, convincing confirmation, and message customization to satisfy the needs and inspirations of the client. The primary objective of convincing correspondence is to accentuate the value and benefits of the great or administration being advanced.

As a delineation, a sales rep is giving a potential client another product item. They give a contextual investigation that shows how the product helped a practically identical firm improve efficiency by 30% as opposed to cudgeling the client with specialized talk. The salesman effectively convinces the client by exhibiting the worth of the item using true models and quantitative outcomes.

•**Handling Rebuttals.** In sales, objections are common and should be viewed as opportunities to calm the client's concerns. Effective objection management necessitates attentive listening, comprehension of the customer's point of view, and prepared and pertinent counterarguments.

Sales reps can foster a relationship of trust and believability with clients by answering complaints in a convenient and proficient way. Model

A potential shopper brings up issues about an item's cost. Accordingly, the sales rep recognizes the concern and underscores the reserve funds for a really long time and profit from the venture that the item gives. They offer additional data as well as declarations from blissful clients who have decreased costs in the wake of utilizing the arrangement. The salesman gets past the client's reservations by tending to the protest and introducing persuading avocation.

•Compelling Cross examination

Compelling addressing is a significant deal of correspondence expertise. By asking intelligent and pertinent questions, salespeople can learn about their customers' needs, issues, and motivations. Clients are bound to answer top to bottom to unassuming requests, which permits the salesman to alter their pitch. Sales reps can more readily get a handle on the requirements of the client and position their item or administration as an answer by utilizing vital addressing. Model, A salesman talks with an expected client about their organization's troubles. What are the biggest difficulties you experience in your current work process?

All things considered, having strong social capacities is principal for bargains since it enables agents to connect with clients, appreciate their requirements, and affect their route. Specialists can also cultivate their social limits and expand their playfulness in deals by means of finishing colossal methods, for example, full concentration, likeness building, solid correspondence, watching out for fights, and sensible tending to. By continually using these frameworks and adjusting them to explicit conditions, bargain specialists may ultimately have the option to lay out additional strong associations, finish up additional arrangements, and eventually advance business improvement. To become capable in these correspondences, practice, examination, and it are crucial for progressing learning. With effort and responsibility, agents can end up finding actual successful communicators and master these capacities, expanding the worth of the necessities of both their associations and clients.

Chapter 6

Building Customer Relationships

These client ties are fundamental for the progress of any affiliation. Positive client relations can be the distinction between an organization that is flourishing and developing and one that is stale and struggling. All in all, what truly do" client relations" number, and what are a few ordinary misinterpretations?

How might you function your client associations with assistance your organization create and flourish?

What does a customer relationship look like?

Simply put, a client connection is the relationship your company has with its customers—including you and your employees. Any customer who purchases labor and products from an organization has a relationship with that organization. client experiences with the organization's public-confronting request(e.g., site or slip-up-and-mortar store) to the client's involvement in the labor and products itself to the drawn out association between the client and business containing this relationship. Something definitive is to lay out a drawn out relationship that will prompt the client copping

an organization's labor and products once more. structure client associations involves laying out and keeping up with attachments with visitors through dispatches or other business procedures that benefit the purchaser." It isn't the business who pays the allowance," Henry Passage said. Businesses simply manage magnates. The client is the person who pays the recruits." Design and reinforcing these associations can prompt high level client standards for dependability, expanded client base through informal exchange and promoting, and expanded client continuation esteem(CLV) — the all out quantum a client is expected to enjoy during their relationship with a business.

For what reason is it important to have strong client associations?

A business is nothing without customers. As indicated by an infamous Vince Lombardi remark," it requires a very long time to track down a client and seconds to lose one." In order to keep existing customers and attract new ones, a business must be able to efficiently serve them and maintain strong client relationships.

Permitting and using criticism, too as compelling correspondence, can emphatically improve the risk that visitors will get back to your affiliation, empowering client devotion. Client devotion is by and large connected with high circumstances of client fulfillment, which incontinently prompts extraordinary circumstances for a foundation and upgraded productivity and development over the long haul.

Five techniques for idealizing client associations
 • Put yourself out there without any problem
 • Request(and answer) client input
 • figure trust
 • Deal with them like people
 • cost loyalty structure more grounded client relations might seem, by all accounts, to be a

sensitive errand, however the ways underneath can assist with working on the cycle.

• Put yourself out there without any problem
Agreeable contact, whether through brilliant pamphlets, follow-up calls, or for sure a periodic registration course book correspondence, is the trendy framework to arrive at visitors and produce long haul associations.

• Request(and answer) client input
It's indispensable to have an open channel of correspondence that permits visitors to give ideas for progressions or varieties. Looking for criticism through a check or different means is one more way to deal with exhibits that you watch about the client experience.

• figure trust
Trust is fundamental for each effective working relationship. Visitors have explicit possibilities regarding quality, promptitude, and thickness. Try not to let them down, and in the event that you do, make sense of what occurred and what transforms you are making to help it from passing once more.

• **Treat them as if they were human guests**—after all, they are living beings who expect to be treated with dignity and respect. Norway failed to remember the individual on the opposite end.

• **Price fidelity Abatements for repeat guests or personality.** Client prices programs can significantly increase the number of customers who stay with you for a long time. Try not to be hesitant to speak with visitors and express your appreciation and an incentive for them.

In summary,Deals units might isolate themselves in a cutthroat territory, advance benefit development, and produce a devout client base by focusing on the making of magnificent client associations. Constant variation and advancement grounded on client criticism will permit ventures to remain in front of the opposition and develop long haul associations with their visitors.

6.1 Promoting Loyalty and Repeat Purchases

In the present very serious organization climate, developing client steadfastness and driving recurrent business are basic for long haul achievement. Gaining new clients might be exorbitant and tedious, thus zeroing in on holding existing clients is more financially savvy. Assembling great connections and developing unwaveringly can bring about recurrent business, more prominent client lifetime worth, and positive verbal exchange references. We'll take a look at the most effective sales strategies and customer retention strategies in this post.

•Familiarity with Client Needs

To cultivate steadfastness and empower rehash business, it is basic to comprehend and address your shoppers' requests appropriately. Find opportunities to find out about their inclinations, issues, and assumptions. You can find out about your clients' buying propensities, side interests, and inspirations by concentrating on their information and criticism. With this data, you can change your administrations and give customized encounters that surpass their assumptions.

•Give Exceptional Client support

Remarkable client assistance is basic in encouraging dependability and rehash business. Guarantee that your outreach group is thoroughly prepared in answering client enquiries, protests, and demands in an ideal and polite way. At each touchpoint, endeavor to give a positive and significant client experience. You might make an enduring impact on clients by exceeding everyone's expectations to address their issues.

•Lay out Connections

Building extraordinary client connections is basic for cultivating dependability. Urge your outreach group to make genuine associations by effectively tuning in, communicating sympathy, and truly thinking often about their requirements. Keep up with normal correspondence and customize your experiences to remain top-of-mind. Normal registrations, customized messages, and virtual entertainment cooperation can all reinforce ties and help clients to remember your value.

•Offer Worth Added Administrations

Offering esteem added administrations is a proficient way to deal with encouraging devotion and drive rehash business. Distinguish new administrations or items that supplement your primary offers and give clients extra advantages. Service agreements, devotion plans, educational assets, and elite limits are instances of these. Esteem added administrations further develop the client experience as well as produce impetuses for clients to work with you later on.

•Solid marking and informing

Marking and informing consistency is basic for building devotion. Verify that your image's qualities, tone, and character are communicated reliably in all client experiences and touchpoints. Keep a predictable and recognizable brand picture across all promoting materials and web-based entertainment posts. Steady informing helps clients in creating trust and devotion over the long run.

•Request Client Input

Looking for and esteeming client input effectively demonstrates your devotion to persistent improvement. Request input consistently through studies, criticism structures, or online assessments. Utilize this input to track down regions for development and to fix any issues quickly. Clients will feel more appreciated and faithful to your image assuming they are engaged with the dynamic interaction.

•Anticipate Client Needs

To increment client steadfastness, attempt to expect their necessities and supply arrangements before they exist. Examine customer data for patterns, trends, and potential issues in the future. Contact clients ahead of time with applicable suggestions or arrangements that address their singular necessities. You might procure certainty and reliability by displaying prescience and giving proactive assistance.

•Really Settle Issues

Botches occur, yet what you address them has a major meaning for the customer unwaveringly. Prioritize immediate and efficient solutions whenever issues arise. Give your sales team the authority to identify issues and offer appropriate solutions as soon as possible. Apologize genuinely, talk transparently, and exceed everyone's expectations to make things right.

Successfully settling concerns shows your commitment to consumer loyalty and can change a negative encounter into a positive one, making unwaveringly and rehashing business.

•Advance Client Support

Clients who are faithful to your image can become significant brand advocates, promoting your items or administrations through informal exchange references. Urge and rouse clients to enlighten others regarding their superb encounters. Carry out client reference programs that remunerate them for alluding new shoppers. Utilize web-based entertainment organizations to spread positive purchaser criticism and energize client produced content. By turning devoted customers into advocates, you can grow your clientele and instill trustworthiness in new customers.

Conclusion

Loyalty and repeat business are two strategic requirements for any sales organization. Understanding client requests, offering remarkable support, making connections, offering esteem added administrations, and continually articulating your image message will assist you with building client unwaveringly. Long-term client loyalty is aided by seeking feedback, rewarding loyalty, anticipating requirements, effectively addressing concerns, and remaining top of mind. You might make extraordinary client connections, increment rehash business, and flourish in a cutthroat economy by applying these procedures and best practices.

6.2 Resolving Complaints and Difficult Situations

Client protests and tough spots are undeniable in the deals business. While these situations might seem scary, they likewise present gigantic potential outcomes to increment client steadfastness, further develop processes, and further develop by and large deals execution. To really determine grievances and predicaments, a mix of compassion, undivided attention, critical abilities to think, and a pledge to client fulfillment is required. Here, we will take a gander at strategies and best practices for managing grumblings and tough spots in deals, so deal experts can transform issues into opportunities for development and achievement.

•Perceiving Client Objections

Understanding the nature and hidden reasons for client disappointment is the most vital phase in really settling objections and testing conditions. Complaints can be brought about by issues with the product, poor customer service, miscommunication, unfulfilled expectations, or even external factors that are beyond the sales professional's control. Deals experts can gain critical experiences into the principal reasons for the issue by effectively paying attention to clients, posing examining inquiries, and feeling for their concerns. This permits them to actually address the troubles more.

•Compassion and mindful tuning in

Undivided attention is a basic expertise for managing objections and predicaments. It involves giving total consideration, keeping in touch, and exhibiting certified interest in grasping the client's perspective. Deals laborers can foster compassion and compatibility with clients by rehearsing undivided attention. Compassion is fundamental since it shows genuine worry for the client's opinions and approves their experience. By acknowledging the customer's feelings and concerns, sales professionals can lay the groundwork for efficient problem resolution.

•**Maintaining Professionalism**. While empathy is essential, maintaining professionalism is also necessary when dealing with complaints and challenging circumstances. Indeed, even in tough spots, deals experts ought to resist the urge to panic, create, and be respectful. It is basic not to think about grumblings literally or to protectively answer. Deals staff can guarantee that the emphasis stays on settling the issue and offering a decent answer for the client by staying proficient.

•Correspondence that is successful

To determine protests and intense conditions, clear and successful correspondence is fundamental. Sales reps ought to convey in a reasonable, respectful, and arrangement centered way. They should make an effort to resolve the client's issues immediately and openly, avoiding technical jargon and ambiguous language that could further confuse or frustrate the customer. Ideal data, normal subsequent meet-ups, and the foundation of reasonable assumptions are basic in creating trust and trust in the settlement cycle.

•Critical thinking and Inventiveness

Settling concerns much of the time requires critical abilities to think and imaginative reasoning. Every situation ought to be drawn closer by salesmen as an opportunity to make effective fixes. They ought to survey the issue genuinely, think about assorted sees, and research conceivable goal decisions. Teaming up with inner groups, getting input from managers or coaches, and conceptualizing thoughts can all assist with delivering effective arrangements that fit both the requirements of the client and the restrictions of the organization.

• **Taking Responsibility and Accountability.**It is essential to develop consumer trust to take responsibility for the situation and hold oneself accountable for the solutions. Salesmen ought to acknowledge liability regarding any mistakes or shortcomings, apologize earnestly, and show a pledge to settling the issue. Sales professionals demonstrate their willingness to go above and beyond to successfully resolve a problem by taking ownership of the situation. This also demonstrates their dedication to providing exceptional customer service.

•**Offering Fair Remuneration or Arrangements**

Now and again, giving reasonable remuneration or arrangements could help with the compelling goal of objections and tough spots. Depending on the nature of the complaint, compensation can take the form of refunds, discounts, replacements, or free goods or services. Deals experts ought to assess the situation and pick the most suitable sort of compensation that is predictable with the client's assumptions and the association's guidelines. In addition to resolving the immediate issue, providing equitable compensation demonstrates the business's commitment to customer satisfaction.

Complaints and difficult situations can be effectively managed and resolved by sales professionals who employ these strategies and best practices, transforming challenges into opportunities for growth and success. At long last, grumbling goal can prompt more grounded client associations, higher client dedication, and further developed deals execution, which benefits both the deals proficient and the association they address.

Chapter 7

Power of Social Media and Digital Communication

The meaning of virtual amusement and high level correspondence on bargains can't be underlined. Over the past ten years, platforms like Facebook, Twitter, Instagram, LinkedIn, and others have become an essential part of people's lives. This has given businesses an unparalleled opportunity to interact, collaborate, and sell their products or services. This paper analyzes the tremendous capacity of electronic amusement and automated correspondence in delivering bargains, displaying the different habits by which they are disturbing the business scene.

•**Extended Reach and Zeroing in on**: One of the fundamental benefits of virtual diversion and modernized correspondence is the ability to contact an enormous and separated swarm.

Regular advancing philosophies had a bound reach since they relied upon expansive correspondences outlets like television or print. Associations, on the other hand, can attract millions, if not billions, of potential clients from one side of the planet to the other through electronic diversion. Advertising methodologies that are more exact and productive can be carried out by focusing on unambiguous socioeconomics and interests. Through broad client profiles and information examination, organizations can customize their informing and content to draw in with their interest group, improving the probability of deals changing.

• **Better relationships with and engagement with customers:** Online diversion stages offer associations an outstanding opportunity to interface clearly with their clients, cultivating a sensation of neighborhood building critical associations. Associations may actually participate in conversations, handle client issues, and give altered organization by using the power of comments, likes, shares, and direct illuminating. This affiliation adds to the progression of trust, commitment, and brand backing, which consequently drives bargains. Besides, social listening plans license relationships to screen brand-related conversations, gaining important data that can coordinate things headway and exhibiting techniques.

•**Amazing powerhouse Promoting and Client Made Content:** Awe-inspiring phenomenon advancing has acquired monster balance in the high level world of late. Forces to be reckoned with, or people with gigantic and dynamic online amusement followings, have emerged as convincing brand delegates. Organizations can showcase their items or administrations by utilizing the believability and reach of forces to be reckoned with through cooperation. Forces to be reckoned with can deliver care and interest in an association by making fair and open substance that resounds with their group. Also, client made material, for instance, client reviews, accolades, and thing shows, abilities as amicable confirmation and helps anticipated clients with securing trust, achieving more critical arrangements.

• **Data analytics and targeted advertising:** Virtual entertainment and advanced correspondence channels can be utilized by organizations to help deals and further develop promoting systems. Companies can gain insight into customer behavior, preferences, and buying habits by utilizing advanced investigation solutions. This information makes it easier to create targeted marketing campaigns that precisely target the right audience with updated messages at the right time. Associations could smooth out their displaying tries, further develop change rates, and intensify the benefit from adventure (profit from introductory capital speculation) by using the power of estimations and machine knowledge.

•**Online business and Steady Trades:** The methodology of online diversion and high level correspondence has blended with the advancement of electronic business. Shopping convenience has been integrated directly into stages like Instagram, Facebook, and Pinterest, allowing associations to sell things or organizations actually. This makes it simpler for clients to find, explore, and purchase things without leaving the web-based entertainment climate. Plus, developments like shoppable posts, chatbots, and secure portion sections have sped up trades and given a more reliable buying experience, achieving extended livelihoods for associations.

• **Continuous Criticism and Market Information**: Considering the speed and snappiness of virtual amusement and high level correspondence stages, associations can get consistent analysis on their things or organizations. By conducting checks, audits, and notices, businesses can easily identify customer satisfaction levels, issues, and growth areas. Organizations can rapidly resolve issues, make ideal changes, and improve their contributions to meet client assumptions because of this speedy criticism circle. Additionally, online amusement networks engage relationships to gain market encounters by following examples, contention development, and customer assessment. This data assists with recognizing creating business area demands, staying before the resistance, and arranging focused bargains techniques.

•Cost-Sufficiency and Benefit from Adventure: When stood out from ordinary promoting procedures, online amusement and high level correspondence offer gigantic cost speculation reserves. Making a profile on an electronic diversion stage is ordinarily free, and associations could run both normal and paid advancing. Paid publicizing through online diversion stages engages firms to contact a greater group at a lower cost than standard advancing procedures. Also, the ability to take apart and evaluate key execution pointers (KPIs) continuously offers affiliations principal encounters into the reasonability of their promoting works out. This data driven approach engages firms to even more capably direct resources, further foster campaigns, and achieve an improved yield on theory (return for cash contributed).

•**Viral Displaying and Improvement**: Online amusement stages have the unmatched capacity to help viral displaying, in which content could spread quickly across networks, delivering basic transparency and responsibility. Attracting, shareable substance can show up at an enormous number of clients in a short period of time, further creating brand detectable quality and the chance of arrangements. To help sharing and responsibility, viral displaying tries could use innovative and entrancing story, astute perspectives, or client made material. These undertakings, when performed well, can create colossal thought, attract new clients, and drive pay advancement.

Online amusement and high level correspondence have changed the arrangements scene, outfitting firms with in advance unbelievable open doors to communicate, attract, and sell. The impact of online amusement and high level correspondence in aiding bargains is unquestionable, from extended reach and obligation to awe-inspiring phenomenon publicizing, data assessment, and progressing analysis. Businesses can unlock enormous sales growth potential by targeting specific demographics, forming meaningful relationships, utilizing user-generated content, and utilizing global markets. In an undeniably associated world, organizations that embrace these advanced channels might adjust, develop, and get by.

7.1 Making Use of Social Media Platforms

We understand the benefit of integrating online entertainment into our showcasing blend as advertisers. Without a doubt, 74% of worldwide advertisers are as yet putting resources into online entertainment showcasing.

In the event that you haven't pondered growing your ongoing web-based entertainment approach, you could be passing up rewarding promoting channels. In this piece, we will give brief clarifications of the worth of online entertainment for business, as well as rundown eight strategies that advertisers can utilize virtual entertainment to accomplish corporate targets.

What is the meaning of web-based entertainment in business?

Assuming you're new to virtual entertainment as a rule, you can sign up for online entertainment confirmation classes to study drawing in and building brand dedication. You will learn how to create a successful social media marketing strategy in these classes, which you will use to transform your company through the power of social media.

Sharing business-related data on your #1 stages will definitely open you to new clients because of the sheer number of clients (3.81 billion to be precise). Driving leads is an immediate result of further developed memorability, and 37% of purchasers say web-based entertainment is the main wellspring of motivation for their buys.

Besides, utilizing online entertainment permits you to develop and sustain your shopper connections. Instead of essentially having a name on their receipts, being dynamic on different stages permits you to speak with clients past their exchanges, showing that you really care about their business.

Considering these perspectives, we should take a gander at eight different ways advertisers could utilize online entertainment to accomplish their business objectives.

8 Social Media Marketing Strategies:
 •Discover Your Personas
•Diverse Channels for Content Promotion
•Maintain High Engagement
 •Provide Customer Service
•Influencer Promotion
•Leads Must Be Nurtured
•Prospecting for Sales
•Display a Different Side of Your Company
•**Discover Your Personas.** If your ultimate

business objective is to learn more about your target markets or customer profiles, you can accomplish this by utilizing a variety of social media platforms. You'll interact with a wide range of people and gain a comprehensive understanding of each audience you have and how to best sell to them because every website has a user base with varying demographics.

For instance, 32.5% of TikTok's client populace is matured 10 to 19, though 33.1% of worldwide Instagram clients are matured 25 to 34. In the event that you own a dress store, you no doubt sell and configure clothing for individuals, everything being equal. Expect you to plan a showcasing methodology for the two stages. All things considered, you'll glean some significant experience about how every one of these segment bunches likes to be promoted to, drawn in with, and what drives the best transformations.

You can utilize virtual entertainment investigation, which gives quantitative insights on your supporters' action and the way that they collaborate with your material. You'll understand what sorts of content every crowd fragment likes and what creates the best changes. Looking further into your clients and what they need makes it more straightforward to configuration fitted adverts that allure for both existing and new clients.

•Advance Substance Through Different Channels

Assuming your organization's just web-based presence is its site, you might be missing out on critical limited time risks that informal communication stages can give. While sites are great for limited time blog passages, virtual entertainment stages might uphold them as well as recordings, photographs, and different kinds of interesting, top notch material. The worth of online entertainment promoting is self-evident, since 58% of advertisers think it has assisted them with expanding deals.

Assuming that you pick along these lines, there are various high-performing destinations where you can offer material to satisfy current shoppers and draw in new ones. Facebook advertising, for instance, can be shown to users who haven't liked your page or commented on its content yet.

It is indispensable to note, nonetheless, that the online entertainment locales you use to advance your material ought to be connected with your organization's general objective. Utilizing TikTok makes no sense if you cater to an older audience because the audience is significantly younger than on other platforms. A business with a more established client base, then again, would profit from utilizing TikTok to drive new leads through special material in the event that you want to expand your online entertainment stages and target new crowds.

In a nutshell, you can market your content on as many social media platforms as you like by experimenting with social media advertising. You are not limited to targeting a specific population like you are with, for instance, email marketing because advertisements on social media can reach people you have not yet contacted or even identified as prospects.

• **Maintain a high position of engagement**

While there are various systems to keep up with your organization's commitment, online entertainment is a horrendous spot to begin on the grounds that these spots have incredibly dynamic stoner bases. Consider the accompanying measurements Facebook guaranteed around1.82 billion diurnal dynamic addicts in the second from last quarter of 2020. On Twitter, there are 187 million worldwide monetizable diurnal dynamic addicts(mDAU). LinkedIn has 675 million yearly dynamic individuals all through the world. The lower accounts with 1,000 followers account for 9.38 of TikTok's average commerce rate across all follower situations. junkies spend an average of 144 sparkles consistently via web-based entertainment. These figures show that every social media platform has the potential to generate significant revenue. Considering that these measurements incorporate worldwide addicts, time region circulation suggests that there will constantly be somebody on the web and prepared to communicate with your tweets, Instagram Stories, and Facebook posts. At the point when you are dynamic via virtual entertainment and stringently execute a showcasing procedure that considers your devotees' advantages, your commitment rates will be major areas of strength for the stay of which stages you use.

•Give client Administration

half of visitors like to work with affiliations that they accept give astounding client administration. 59 percent of social media drug users around the world are pleased with brands' social media responses to customer service inquiries. Considering this, the upsides of utilizing virtual entertainment to give exceptional client administration are colossal as far as surpassing client possibilities. You can give client care via virtual entertainment in different ways, comparable as answering to client ventures on Twitter or talking with them on Facebook Courier. Then, at that point, is a representation of a wreck conveyance membership administration, HelloFresh, involving Twitter for client support. You can utilize your social accounts to share supportive associations with client issues that bring about expansion to answering questions. various ventures have learned through the new client administration turn to limit activity client administration that visitors appreciate being made uncertain of undertakings somewhat early as opposed to finding them all alone. They esteem clarity, and online entertainment is a phenomenal stage for proliferating this data. In all actuality, this could mean illuminating buyers early on about certain delivery confinements through Twitter or distributing an Instagram Story illuminating diner supporters that you've shut your restaurant ahead of time because of startling conditions. Social media management systems like Sprout Social can assist you in ensuring that you always provide excellent customer service. Advertisers might follow client backing questions across all virtual entertainment stages utilizing the help's web-based entertainment client care capacity. Sow Social interfaces with HubSpot Administration Center, permitting you to speak with administration delegates and incontinently move client administration tickets as they show up. A Facebook-generated Service Mecca helpdesk ticket is depicted in the image below.

• Virtual Entertainment Showcasing

As indicated by 71% of advertisers, the nature of visitors and business made by force to be reckoned with promoting is better than other declaration designs. The return on investment (ROI) for every dollar spent on influencers is $5.78. In synopsis, powerhouse showcasing happens when an organization teams up with a powerhouse, or somebody who's widely respected and confided in by their devotees, to deliver a declaration or piece of content. The thing of these coordinated efforts is for each side to gain new visitors from the other stoner base and convert devotees to make a particular move, comparable as copping

an item or administration. While force to be reckoned with promoting through visitor bloggers is wide on sites, utilizing virtual entertainment to go into the universe of powerhouse showcasing is productive, especially on Instagram. Then is a representation of Instagram powerhouse showcasing with music craftsman Amine advancing a coordinated effort with a b-ball detachment. Despite the fact that Amine is a VIP, powerhouse promoting should likewise be possible with miniature powerhouses, web-based entertainment forces to be reckoned with, and assessment pioneers on the off chance that their advantages concur with your image. Expect you to partake in a beauty care products organization. You ought to join with a notable powerhouse in that gathering, comparative as a skincare master or a day to day existence blogger. The association is logically appropriate, and the addicts they would draw into your profile are probably going to be keen on what you bring to the table.

•Foster Leads

With regards to lead support, most extreme advertisers guess dispatch, however it's by all accounts not the only choice. Considering that 96% of guide guests are great, however not yet prepared toward purchase, online entertainment showcasing can significantly prop your endeavors to develop new leads. You can give an assortment of data on your virtual entertainment detects that tends to visitors at bright phases of the purchaser's excursion, which is the cycle that customers go through prior to settling on an ultimate conclusion to make a purchase and come to a client. You can foster educational material for top-of-the-divert visitors in the care stage, comparable as brief web-based entertainment posts, and lower part-of-the-direct happiness for junkies in the buying stage, comparable as Instagram videos of item exhibits.

•Prospecting for Deals

In the wake of related drives, you can join with the arrangements workforce via virtual entertainment to find possibilities from those leads and attempt to change them into paying visitors. During this process, you can train deal representatives to use social listening tools from social media intelligence. Social listening is the design of covering your organization's online entertainment networks for immediate and roundabout brand specifications utilizing relevant watchwords. This permits them to gather data about how possibilities communicate with your online entertainment spots. Oktopost, an online entertainment activity, can be utilized to do virtual entertainment bargains testing. You might utilize online entertainment information to create heart to heart designated promoting juggernauts by following how possibilities communicate with your organization. The deal dispatch-nurturing channel shown in the image below is one that Oktopost can integrate with the HubSpot Content Management System.

•Show an Alternate Side of Your Organization actually, utilize online entertainment to introduce a valid part of your organization and broadcast in the background content, If you need to draw in with your followership in new ways.

In the background content acculturated your foundation to your followership by exhibiting the existence pattern of the item or administration that your affiliation sells. It can accentuate your image's own character and give addicts with data about individuals who make the impacts they revere. Visitors value this sort of material, especially on TikTok. The stage is by and large utilized by Age Z, who esteem credibility in promoting over the average arrangements to-lead methodology. In any case, utilizing the stage can help you in broadening your substance type, showing a new, In the event that your image or business for the most part distributes bargains driven proper substance.

One of a kind Stock Save, a bitsy style foundation, gains by TikTok's advantage in the background material by continually posting flicks displaying their assembling cycle. They occasionally accept requests and post videos of the design process for clothing with supporting details. Their presentation tape had 39.3 K perspectives, and their most famous tape second has north of 26 million perspectives. An example of their before-the-scenes content is displayed in the tape underneath. In general, traditional content that is driven by deals is fine, and marketers are aware that it works. In any case, as Age Z develops and gains the ability to make buys all alone, figuring out how to actuate content that fulfills and tempts them to purchase can put your foundation for progress.

Promoting your business through social media can be beneficial.

There are innumerable styles to utilize virtual entertainment to satisfy your general business assumptions, whether you need to grow your client administration channels or use force to be reckoned with advertising. In any case, your organization will probably acquire from utilizing online entertainment, Assuming you go out of the way to foster stage explicit showcasing strategies. There are endless styles to utilize virtual entertainment to satisfy your general business assumptions, whether you need to grow your client administration channels or use force to be reckoned with advertising.

7.2 Engaging Customers through Content Marketing

Content promoting has developed as a critical technique for associations to connect with clients on and increment deals in the present computerized climate. Customary deals approaches are losing viability, and purchasers currently anticipate that organizations should give fascinating and pertinent data. By producing and disseminating high-quality content that resonates with their target audience, businesses can build trust, establish thought leadership, and ultimately drive consumer engagement through content marketing. Here, we will take a gander at how to connect with clients involving content showcasing in deals,. like characterizing your crowd, creating engaging substance, utilizing various channels, and estimating achievement.

•**Figuring out the segment**: To connect with clients successfully through happy promoting, associations should initially recognize their objective segment. Leading statistical surveying and evaluating client socioeconomics, ways of behaving, and inclinations are all essential for this. Organizations can create content that answers the singular requirements of their clients by understanding their torment spots, hardships, and objectives. This redid technique ensures that the material resounds with the crowd, catches their eye, and rouses them to act.

•**Making Spellbinding Substance:** The foundation of successful content marketing is captivating content. It is basic to produce content for the main interest group that is important, educational, and locking in. The data ought to bear some significance with them and give answers for their challenges. Blog articles, infographics, recordings, digital broadcasts, and digital books are incredible substance types. Organizations might increment commitment by taking care of different learning styles and inclinations by utilizing various arrangements.

•Utilizing Different Channels: To improve the scope and effect of content showcasing exercises, it is basic to utilize different channels to disperse and advance the material. Long range informal communication networks like Facebook, Twitter, LinkedIn, and Instagram permit you to post content and associate with clients straightforwardly. Organizations can utilize email showcasing to support prospects and lay out a customized association with clients. Likewise, visitor posting on applicable industry locales and drawing in with powerhouses could help the substance contact new crowds.

• Individualization and Modification: In the present swarmed advanced market, personalisation and customization are basic to client commitment. Organizations can give a more customized insight by adjusting data to specific client inclinations, supporting the chances of commitment and change. This can be achieved by using information investigation, division, and computerization apparatuses, which empower associations to foster custom-made content in view of client ways of behaving, interests, and past connections.

•**Visual and interactive content**: Utilizing content showcasing to connect with clients frequently requires going past run of the mill text-based designs. Using interactive and visual content like quizzes, polls, surveys, and interactive films can catch and keep customers' attention. These structures advance dynamic support and give a more vivid encounter, advancing commitment and brand dependability. Integrating stylishly engaging elements, like great photos, infographics, and recordings, can likewise work on the general allure and shareability of the data.

•**Storytelling:** Narrating is a strong substance promoting strategy that can draw in clients and evoke close to home connections. By developing narratives that resonate with their target audience, businesses can create an experience that is both memorable and engaging. Stories help to adapt brands, assemble close to home associations with clients, and make content really convincing. Sharing client examples of overcoming adversity, contextual investigations, and in the background brand looks are extraordinary strategies to incorporate narrating into content advertising.

•**Website design enhancement and Content Advancement:** Making intriguing substance is essentially one part of the riddle. It is basic to improve content for web crawlers to ensure that it arrives at its ideal interest group. Watchword research, on-page streamlining, and external link establishment are instances of site design improvement (Website optimization) that can work on the perceivability of material in web search tool results. By incorporating relevant keywords, enhancing meta tags, and guaranteeing a user-friendly website experience, businesses can increase organic traffic and attract customers who are actively seeking information about their products or services. Content streamlining likewise incorporates coordinating the substance so it is effectively intelligible and searchable, with the utilization of headings, list items, and subheadings to further develop the client experience.

•**Consistency and Recurrence:** Content improvement should be predictable and regular to draw in clients. Distributing new and important substances consistently permits firms to remain top of psyche with their ideal interest group. It lays out validity and authority while likewise uplifting clients to return for extra data. Making a substance schedule and adhering to a steady distributing plan gives clients a reason to cooperate with the organization consistently. It is, all things considered, basic to accomplish a harmony among amount and quality. While continuous material updates are worthwhile, keeping up with great principles ought not be forfeited.

•**Engaging Clients**: Content promoting is something other than creating and disseminating content. It likewise involves effectively captivating clients to lay out a feeling of local area and invigorate association. This can be achieved by answering remarks and messages via virtual entertainment, coordinating online courses or live back and forth discussions, and taking part in important industry gatherings or online networks. Drawing in with clients empowers associations to make connections, handle objections, and get valuable criticism, eventually expanding client reliability and backing.

•**Estimating Achievement**: To assess the success of their content marketing efforts, businesses must monitor key performance indicators (KPIs). Site traffic, virtual entertainment cooperation, change rates, time spent on page, and lead age are famous measurements to screen. Organizations might comprehend which kinds of content are drawing in with their crowds and adjust their methodology as needed by contemplating these examinations. To sufficiently quantify accomplishment, exact objectives and benchmarks should be laid out. Besides, gathering criticism through studies and client tributes can give subjective bits of knowledge into the effect of content showcasing on buyer commitment and deals.

•**Ceaseless Transformation and Advancement**: The field of content marketing is one that is always changing and requires constant adaptation and development. Firms must adapt to remain competitive because customer preferences, technological advancements, and market trends are constantly shifting. It is basic to assess and change content promoting strategies on a successive premise in light of execution measurements and client criticism. Watching out for creating patterns and new satisfied structures can likewise prompt new strategies to enhance and connect with clients.

Conclusion: In the present deals climate, content advertising is a successful procedure for connecting with clients and helping deals. Organizations can have areas of strength for assembling, lay out thought administration, and eventually convert leads into steadfast clients by figuring out their crowd, giving convincing substance, utilizing various channels, customizing the experience, and observing execution. The goal is to produce high-quality, useful, and engaging content that addresses the preferences and requirements of the intended audience. Organizations might remain on the ball and make long haul progress in drawing in clients and driving deals through satisfied showcasing by continually changing and advancing their substance advertising techniques.

Conclusion

From Words to Sales - Your Path to Success.
To sum up, the way from words to deals is a changing one that includes a careful comprehension of effective correspondence, convincing methodologies, and a client driven mentality. We saw that the force of words can really influence the progress of any association or individual all through this examination.

Misjudging the worth of clear and direct communication is inconceivable. The ability to effectively convey a message, whether through composed content, vocal introductions, or relational experiences, is basic in grabbing the eye and interest of likely clients. People and undertakings might construct areas of strength for a for deals accomplishment by excelling at composing convincing stories, underlining novel selling recommendations, and settling shopper torment regions.

Besides, the specialty of influence is crucial to changing words into deals. Figuring out human brain science, inspirations, and dynamic cycles empowers us to modify our messages and requests to our ideal interest group's inclinations. We can convince clients to act and make a buy by utilizing profound requests, social evidence, and legitimate thinking. Influence power lies in the capacity to convince, yet additionally in the capacity to foster long haul associations with clients in light of trust and validity.

A client centered procedure is basic to deal with achievement. In today's highly competitive industry, customers have more options than ever before. Therefore, figuring out their needs, inclinations, and agony spots is basic to make tweaked arrangements that satisfy their assumptions. Organizations that embrace a client driven approach can have areas of strength for fostering reliability, and make brand champions who won't just rehash buys yet in addition allude others to the organization.

The street from words to deals isn't without its challenges. Consistent learning, flexibility, and a preparation to embrace new procedures and innovation are required. The deals scene is steadily changing, and remaining on the ball is basic. Organizations should embrace advancement and use arising patterns to stay serious in the commercial center, from bridling the force of online entertainment and computerized showcasing to utilizing information examination and computerization.

At last, the way to deal with achievement is a particular and unmistakable excursion for every person and company. It requires a combination of expertise, creativity, tenacity, and knowledge. The objective is to move toward the cycle with fervor, energy, and a receptive outlook.

Acknowledge disappointment as learning an open door, continually change your procedures, and look constantly for ways of getting to the next level.

From Words to Deals - Your Way to Progress
is a book that will help people and organizations explore the troublesome universe of deals. Perusers might increment deals and accomplish their ideal level of progress by getting a handle on the force of words, learning the specialty of influence, and taking on a client driven methodology.

Deals achievement is resolved by what you say, yet additionally by how you say it and to whom you say it. It is tied in with connecting on a more profound level with clients, figuring out their necessities, and giving arrangements that really work on their lives. People and organizations might change their words into significant deals and clear their approach to long haul accomplishment by following the thoughts introduced in this aide.